GREAT CAREERS IN
WRITING

by Brienna Rossiter

FOCUS
READERS.
NAVIGATOR

WWW.FOCUSREADERS.COM

Focus Readers is distributed by North Star Editions:
sales@northstareditions.com | 888-417-0195

Produced for Focus Readers by Red Line Editorial.

Photographs ©: Shutterstock Images, cover, 1, 4–5, 7, 11, 13, 14–15, 17, 19, 20–21, 23, 25, 26–27; iStockphoto, 8–9; Red Line Editorial, 29

Library of Congress Cataloging-in-Publication Data
Names: Rossiter, Brienna, author.
Title: Great careers in writing / by Brienna Rossiter.
Description: Lake Elmo, MN : Focus Readers, [2022] | Series: Great careers | Includes index. | Audience: Grades 4-6
Identifiers: LCCN 2021008306 (print) | LCCN 2021008307 (ebook) | ISBN 9781644938508 (hardcover) | ISBN 9781644938966 (paperback) | ISBN 9781644939420 (ebook) | ISBN 9781644939840 (pdf)
Subjects: LCSH: Authorship--Vocational guidance--Juvenile literature.
Classification: LCC PN153 .R67 2022 (print) | LCC PN153 (ebook) | DDC 808.02023--dc23
LC record available at https://lccn.loc.gov/2021008306
LC ebook record available at https://lccn.loc.gov/2021008307

Printed in the United States of America
Mankato, MN
082021

ABOUT THE AUTHOR

Brienna Rossiter is a writer and editor who lives in Minnesota. She enjoys reading many kinds of writing but especially likes stories that involve mysteries.

TABLE OF CONTENTS

CHAPTER 1

SHARING STORIES

When most people think of writers, they often think of famous novelists. But for those who are interested in writing, there are many career options besides writing books. Writers create and share their work in a variety of ways.

For example, some people write for magazines or newspapers. Reporters

Reporters work for a variety of news outlets, including newspapers, websites, and TV shows.

research stories and events. They often specialize in certain topics, such as sports or politics. Columnists share their opinions. They write on a schedule, such as once a week. Some give advice. Others focus on current events.

Other writers publish their own work. People often share their work on social

COMICS

Comics use words and pictures together to tell stories. Short comics may have just one or two drawings. Graphic novels can have hundreds of pages. Sometimes one person does both the writing and the art. But it's common for people to work on teams. A writer creates the story. Then an artist creates the drawings.

Authors sometimes hold events at bookstores. They read from their books and meet their fans.

media, too. They post recipes, opinions, advice, and more. These creators can become very famous. Sometimes **publishers** ask them to write books.

CHAPTER 2

JOBS IN PUBLISHING

Some people choose to publish books on their own. However, creating a book usually involves more people than just the author. For example, authors often work with literary agents. Agents help authors send their work to publishers. That way, authors can find publishers that want to produce their books.

A literary agent receives hundreds of submissions every year from people who want to be authors.

At traditional publishing companies, several kinds of editors are involved in creating books. The process often starts with acquisitions editors. These people help choose which books the company will buy and publish.

If a book gets chosen, it goes to a developmental editor. This person suggests ways to make the book better. This step focuses on large-scale changes, such as the book's pacing or plot. After these revisions, the book goes to a copy editor. This person looks at each sentence and paragraph. The copy editor makes sure words are used well. Other people may read the book, too. For example, if

A developmental editor may speak to an author to discuss ideas for improving a book.

the book is nonfiction, a fact-checker makes sure the information is accurate.

When the text is ready, book designers get it ready to print. Then, when the book is almost done, it goes to a proofreader.

This person looks for small errors before the book is printed.

A marketing team helps sell the book. This team often helps choose the book's title. Its members also plan the cover and **blurb**. They try to make people interested

TRANSLATORS

Translators help change writing from one language to another. They try to make the new version as close to the original as possible. They try to match both the meaning and the writing style. This process can be especially tricky for creative writing. Translators speak at least two languages. They often translate into their native language. That helps them get slang or figures of speech right.

Reviewers write about more than just books. They also write about concerts, movies, plays, and more.

in buying the book. They may also send the book to booksellers and reviewers.

A reviewer writes about books other people publish. Reviewers share what they did and didn't like. They often say whether they would recommend a book to others. As a result, reviewers can greatly influence how well books sell.

CHAPTER 3

DRAFTING DOCUMENTS

Some writers help companies prepare documents. These writers often do research. They also follow rules about **format** and writing style. Proposal writers help their companies get **contracts**. They explain what their companies can do. And they explain how their companies would complete certain projects.

Proposal writers create documents that help businesses get new projects or make sales.

Grant writers help some organizations get money. They send proposals to donors. Each proposal must follow rules for length and the order of information. Also, the proposal must be persuasive. Writers try to convince donors to give money to their organizations.

SPEECHWRITERS

Speechwriters plan what people will say at important events. They often work for politicians or other famous people. Speechwriters plan how to best meet the speaker's goals. They think about what message the speaker wants to send. And they consider how listeners might react. They choose words that will create the desired effect.

Technical writers at software companies may work with the coders who created the software.

Technical writers explain how to do or use things. They create instructions and manuals. The text may tell how to put something together. Or it may explain how to use a machine. Technical writers must clearly explain each step.

SCREENWRITERS

Screenwriters create stories for visual media. This includes TV shows and movies. People also write screenplays for commercials and video games.

Screenwriters plan what happens in a story. They develop the characters. And they write the dialogue. Some screenwriters write their own stories. Others adapt stories based on books.

A screenwriter's script follows a certain format. Some parts describe where the action takes place. Other parts show which character is speaking.

To become screenwriters, people study writing. They also work to meet others in the industry. Screenwriters often get jobs through their connections. So, screenwriters may move to cities where lots of movies or TV shows are made.

Many screenwriters live in Los Angeles, California. Numerous TV shows and movies are made there.

CHAPTER 4

JOBS IN BUSINESS

Many writers and editors help companies communicate with employees and customers. For instance, most large companies have a communications department. This department handles how the company sends out information. The information can take many forms, including emails

A communications team helps decide what information to send out about the company.

and newsletters. Some are sent out to customers. Others are for the company's employees. People in communications write and edit each one.

Copywriters help companies sell goods and services. They write text for blogs, websites, advertisements, and social media. A content strategist is often involved. This person plans how the company will use its website and other online content.

Strategists try to make this content useful and interesting to readers. They also look at how the content can improve the company's sales. To do this, they must understand advertising and **analytics**.

Many companies hire copywriters to create the content on their websites.

A content marketer often works closely with the content strategist. While the strategist focuses on defining the company's goals, the marketer focuses on how to meet them. Together, they decide what content to post and where to post it. Marketers help the company attract attention. For example, they might write a series of blog posts. Some posts may promote the company directly. Other posts may focus more on things customers enjoy.

Similarly, social media specialists use social media to reach a company's goals.

PUBLIC RELATIONS

Jobs in public relations (PR) focus on helping a company or client have a good image. People in PR learn ways to stop harmful information from spreading. They try to attract positive attention instead. PR workers send out **press releases**. They write posts and give speeches. And they encourage other people to say good things about their client or company.

Social media specialists must know how to use many different platforms.

For example, they may try to attract a certain number of followers. They track what ideas and content are successful. And they plan what to post in the future. They also interact with customers through posts and comments.

CHAPTER 5

ENTERING THE FIELD

Some people who work in writing teach themselves. They send companies samples of their work. They get jobs based on their skills or experience. But for many writing jobs, people must attend college. They usually study English, journalism, communications, or a related field. Some also study the field of the

College helps prepare students for a wide variety of writing careers.

organizations they hope to work for. For instance, grant writers may learn about nonprofits.

Writing jobs can be very competitive. Many people start as **interns**. They often work for little or no pay. But they build skills and experience. That way, they can get more advanced jobs later on.

Many writers **freelance**. They may work for more than one company. And they may do several different jobs. Having a variety of skills is helpful in publishing. That's because many people apply for each job. So, a person with many skills will stand out. Marketing and social media skills are especially useful.

Very few people become famous authors. Even so, there are plenty of other great careers in writing. Many writers find jobs that are both challenging and enjoyable.

CAREER PREP CHECKLIST

Interested in a career in writing? As you move into middle school and high school, try these steps.

1 Read lots of different genres, especially examples of the kind of writing you want to do.

2 Study the rules of editing and grammar. Also, do lots of practice writing.

3 Tell your school's guidance counselor about your interest. This person can help you find opportunities to get experience in writing.

4 Work on your school's newspaper, or find places where new writers can submit their work for free.

5 Look for an organization where you can intern or volunteer to gain experience.

6 Find a critique group where you can share your writing and get tips.

FOCUS ON
GREAT CAREERS IN WRITING

Write your answers on a separate piece of paper.

1. Write a paragraph explaining the steps that are usually involved in publishing a book.

2. Would you rather have a job related to publishing or communications? Why?

3. Which job focuses on helping authors find a company that will publish their books?

   A. literary agent
   B. content marketer
   C. reviewer

4. Why might technical writers work with engineers?

   A. They can tell the engineers what to do.
   B. They can explain how to use the machines that engineers make.
   C. They can convince the engineers to trade jobs.

Answer key on page 32.

GLOSSARY

analytics
Making decisions by studying data and finding patterns.

blurb
Text that gives a short description of a book, usually found on the back cover.

contracts
Agreements where one person or group agrees to do something for another, often in exchange for payment.

format
A particular way of organizing information.

freelance
To do jobs for several different companies instead of working just one position.

interns
People who are new to a field and work for little or no pay as a way to gain experience.

press releases
Documents that are sent to the media to make announcements or give important information.

publishers
Companies that put out books, magazines, or other written materials.

TO LEARN MORE

BOOKS

Dale, Andrew. *Graphic Novels*. Minneapolis: Abdo
    Publishing, 2017.

Hammelef, Danielle S. *Behind-the-Scenes Movie Careers*.
    North Mankato, MN: Capstone Press, 2017.

Harris, Duchess, and Tammy Gagne. *Richard Wright:
    Author and World Traveler*. Minneapolis: Abdo
    Publishing, 2020.

NOTE TO EDUCATORS

Visit **www.focusreaders.com** to find lesson plans,
activities, links, and other resources related to this title.

INDEX

Answer Key: 1. Answers will vary; **2.** Answers will vary; **3.** A; **4.** B